A Children's Book of Morals

Series II

by

Marva L. Boatman

Illustrations by Asim Wilson

Boat-man Enterprises Inc., United States
M. Boatman Publishing
P.O. Box 301
Ladysmith, Virginia 22501

Boatman, Marva L., *A Children's Book of Morals*

Copyright © 2022 by Marva L. Boatman.
All rights reserved.

No part of this book may be reproduced in any form or by any electronic or mechanical means, including information storage and retrieval systems, without written permission from the author, except for use of brief quotations in a book review.

ISBNs: 9780978686512   paperback
       9780978686529   e-book

Library of Congress Control Number: 2023902073

Illustrations by Asim Wilson

Boat-man Enterprise, Inc.
M Boatman Publishing
P O Box 301
Ladysmith, VA 22501
804-647-5490
seriesii050@gmail.com

Printed in the United States of America

Second Printing

Dedicated to the wisdom of our mother
Mrs. Rosa Lee Boatman
1923-1994

Contents

Purpose	i
Vocabulary	ii
Always Tell the Truth	1
Child's Drawings or Comments	2
Obey and Respect Your Parents	3
Child's Drawings or Comments	4
Be Kind	5
Child's Drawings or Comments	6
Doing and Saying the Right Thing	7
Child's Drawings or Comments	8
Thank you	9
Child's Drawings or Comments	10
Please	11
Child's Drawings or Comments	12
Ask Questions	13
Child's Drawings or Comments	14
Love God, Yourself, and Others	15
Child's Drawings or Comments	16
No Drugs, No Alcohol	17
Child's Drawings or Comments	18
Responsibility	19
Child's Drawings or Comments	20
Rewards	21
Child's Drawings or Comments	22
Notes	23-24

Purpose

***For mothers, fathers,
families, and all children***

Parents and adults should read this book with their children:

- + To help children understand these ideas as they relate to their life experience.

- + To help children develop appropriate behavior towards themselves, one another and adults.

- + To assist children in developing character.

- + To encourage discussion of morals, values, and social skills.

Vocabulary

Child's Drawings or Comments

What is a moral?

A moral relates to principles of right and wrong behavior.

A moral is when you learn a valuable lesson from an experience or from a story that teaches you to conduct yourself in the right manner.

What is character?

Character is moral excellence and firmness.

What is spiritual?

Spiritual is knowing and recognizing God's existence as a part of each individual.

Always Tell the Truth

Mother: "Sabin, did you finish you homework last night?
Sabin: 'Yes Mother."
Mother: "Let me review it."
Sabin: "I've already put it in my backpack."

Mother: "Sabin, you must complete your homework and learn to tell the truth about situations."

Child's Drawings or Comments

Obey and Respect Your Parents

It is important to obey your parents for they provide you with guidance and direction to help you gain understanding about God, people, and life.

Child's Drawings or Comments

Be Kind

For it is true...what goes around comes around. You reap what you sow.

We get what we earn. Be kind to yourself and others.

Treat them the way you want to be treated.

"Good morning Marty, how are you?"

"Don't speak to me this morning!"

Child's Drawings or Comments

Doing and Saying the Right Thing

When we enter a store or a building, we walk.

Child's Drawings or Comments

Thank You

When someone gives us something, we say, "Thank you."

Child's Drawings or Comments

Please

When we ask for something, we say, "Please."

Child's Drawings or Comments

Ask Questions

When we want to know about something, we ask questions.

Child's Drawings or Comments

Love God, Family, Yourself, and Other People

We are all spiritual beings.
God is a part of us and we are a part of God.

Child's Drawings or Comments

No Drugs, No Alcohol

Be responsible for your own behavior.

My parents and family: We talk about drugs, alcohol, and other foreign substances. They say these are bad for me and will cause me to fail in life. Using alcohol and drugs will cause me to have problems that I otherwise would not have if I didn't use them.

Child's Drawings or Comments

Responsibility

Be responsible for your behavior. Say to yourself:

I am responsible, therefore I complete my homework everyday.

I am responsible, therefore I complete my chores.

I am responsible, therefore I must learn self-control.

I am responsible, therefore I must learn that I can't have my way all the time.

I am responsible, therefore when I am disciplined for doing the wrong thing or actions, I must learn to be responsible and accept the consequences.

I am responsible, therefore I am able to have talks, listen, and discussions toward good outcomes.

Name: _____

Child's Drawings or Comments

Rewards

- When I practice telling the truth, I develop honesty within myself.

- When I obey and respect my parents, I learn to respect myself and others.

- When I am kind to others, kindness comes to me.

- When I learn to do and say the right things, I care about myself and others.

- When I love God, family, myself, and others, I am beginning to understand life.

- When I work towards practicing and understanding morals, I am growing towards a good life, character, freedom, and peace.

Marva L. Boatman
Author

Child's Drawings or Comments

Notes

Notes

www.ingramcontent.com/pod-product-compliance
Lightning Source LLC
Chambersburg PA
CBHW062107290426
44110CB00022B/2737